Animal Alphabet

by Gill Davies

illustrated by Gill Guile

Animal Alphabet

An alphabet is all the letters
We can use for words,
And animals are lots of things
From kangaroos to birds.

Animals have names, of course
With lots of letters in,
These poems are invented
On how their names begin.

There is A for Ant and B for Bear
And D for Dinosaur;
L for Lion and N for Newt
And many, many more.

The alphabet has letters
That add up to twenty-six,
So that is how many animals
Are in this rhyming mix.

I hope you like the animals
And all the poems too;
I wonder now – what is your name?
What letters make up you?

A a

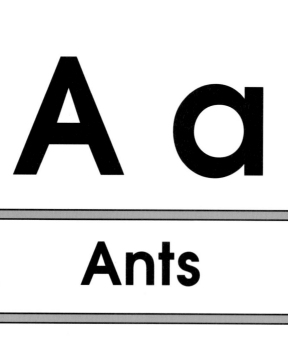

Ants

Ants, ants, ants,
Ants are very strong,
Maybe you have watched one
As he pulls a crumb along.

Now if an ant were human
Or so I have been told,
He could pick up a piano
If you gave him one to hold.

B b

Bears

The grizzly and the polar bears
Were friendly as can be,
So they ate their lunch together
With a sandwich on each knee.

The polar had a white coat,
The grizzly bear's was brown.
They chose the bread that matched them,
Then spread honey up and down.

Now if I were a polar bear
I'd always choose white bread.
But Mother makes me eat the brown
With honey thinly spread.

C c

Crocodile

The little baby crocodile
Was crying by the River Nile.
``No one will be friends with me
Once my great big teeth they see.''
Sharp and gleaming, pointed, white,
His teeth they were a frightening sight.

``I cannot talk, I cannot smile,
Once I do, they run a mile.
No one here will play with me
In case I eat them for my tea!
It's lonely sitting by the Nile,
I'm sad that I'm a crocodile.''

D d

Dinosaurs

Dinosaurs lived long ago
When the world was almost new;
Some were built like buses,
Some had wings and flew.

Diplodocus dinosaurs
Had long, long necks and tails;
They weighed about ten tons or so
When they stepped upon the scales.

If you could have some dinosaurs
To live with you as pets,
It would be hard to keep them in a box
When you took them to the vets.

E e

Elephants

``Elephants eat an enormous amount!''
The zoo keeper grumbled one day.
``From the moment when
I put food in the pen,
Everything's gobbled away.''

The elephants soon were as fat as balloons,
They rolled over and hiccupped all day;
Waving trunks in the air,
They said, ``We don't care;
We are fat and we're staying that way!

``No diets for us; who cares for such fuss?
And who do you think is in charge?
Let the keeper complain,
Let's have pudding again,
Elephants ought to be large!''

F f

Flamingo

A flamingo is a funny bird
Whose shape is really quite absurd,
His neck is long just like a snake
And legs so thin you'd think they'd break;
His beak is twisted in a curve,
He really is a most odd bird!

When Alice goes to Wonderland
Flamingos hide, I understand,
In case she turns them upside down
And swings them up and swings them down;
It makes flamingos feel quite sick
And sore, to be a croquet stick.

But when they have their get-togethers,
Flamingos wear their best pink feathers;
They gather close, then poise for flight
And rise into the soft twilight.
They seem to blush as off they fly
In rosy clouds across the sky.

G g

Giraffe

I'd like to be a tall giraffe
And stretch up to the sky,
Then I could see beyond the trees
And watch the stars go by.

It must be very lonely though
Up there so very high;
I wonder if that's why giraffes
Seem really rather shy.

H h

Hippo

Henry the Hippo was horribly hoarse
From having a hideous cold;
He grumbled, he growled, he huskily howled
But wouldn't do as he was told.

``Go to bed,'' begged his mother.
``Or have a mud bath.''
Said the doctor, ``At least take a pill.''
But Henry just croaked, ``I can't do a thing,
I'm feeling too terribly ill.''

He coughed and he spluttered,
He sneezed and he wheezed,
But he said, as his temperature rose,
``Just leave me alone, I'll sit here and moan
With a clip on the end of my nose!''

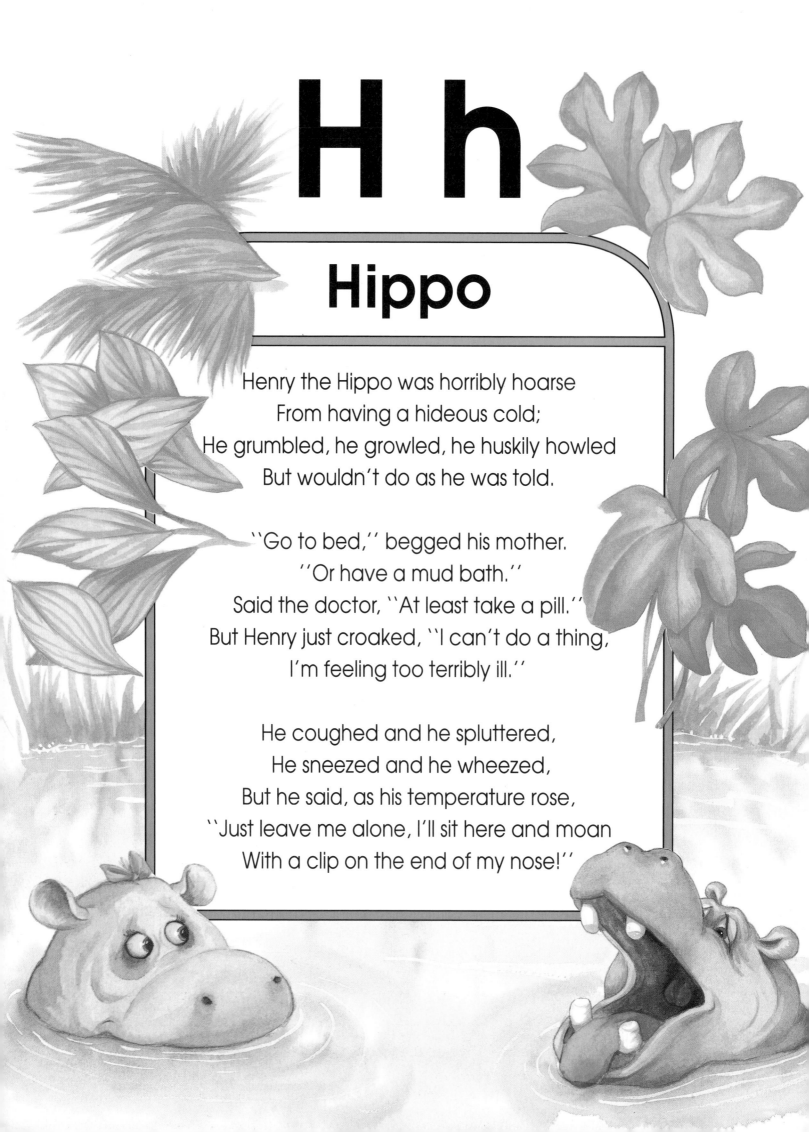

I i

Insect

Hello, Mr Insect,
I'm glad I'm not you,
Having six legs must be difficult
It's bad enough with two!

My legs are always falling over,
They tangle, twist and trip;
I'd never manage six legs
How often do you slip?

And dressing in the morning,
Searching through the drawer,
It's hard to find two socks that match
I'd never find four more.

J j

Jellyfish

Jellyfish are squidgy,
Jellyfish can sting;
Some look just like plastic bags
And some have purple rings.

Jellyfish have tentacles,
Some shine and glow at night;
If on the sea bed I should sleep
They'd be my night-time light.

K k

Kangaroo

A kangaroo collected stones
And kept them in her pouch,
She had so many heavy ones
She soon began to slouch.

There were rounded, red and stripey ones
And shiny black ones too,
And some that looked like glass or gold
And others speckled blue.

Soon kangaroo was so weighed down
She found she couldn't jump;
Each time she tried to walk or bounce
The stones went thumpy-bump!

So kangaroo called all her friends
And gave them each a stone,
She said, ``Please put this in your pouch for me
And take it to my home.''

L l

Lion

The lazy lion lazed about
And sat upon his bottom;
He didn't wash his tail or mane
For fear that it would rot 'em.

He didn't lick or comb his ears
Or keep his whiskers neat,
Until they tried to sweep him up
Into the garbage heap.

``Hey, don't do that!'' he cried in fear,
``It's me, the lazy lion!''
And off he rushed to scrub his mane
And give his tail an iron.

So now he soaks in hot, hot pools
Until his coat is gleaming;
It's not a forest fire you see,
It's just the lion, steaming.

M m

Monkey

There are many sorts of monkey
Of every shape and size,
I like the woolly monkey best
He looks so kind and wise.

His fur is soft, like velvet,
So thick and dark and deep;
His eyes are round as saucers,
He can run and swing and leap.

There are many sorts of monkey,
Some are tiny, some are tall;
But I think the woolly monkey
Is the nicest one of all.

N n

Newt

The new newt knew what the new newt knew,
He knew where the new weeds newly grew;
He knew where the dragonflies flying flew,
The new newt knew what the new newt knew.

The new newt knew what the new newt knew,
He knew where the dewy grass dewily grew;
He knew where the butterflies flying flew,
The new newt knew what the new newt knew.

Octopus

When an octopus gives you a hug
It really is quite a delight,
She has so many loving arms
To wrap around you tight.

So when you need some comforting
Because life is in a muddle,
Just call on Mrs Octopus –
She's a sucker for a cuddle!

P p

Penguin

Percy and Polly were penguins
Who lived where the seas are ice;
Now they both loved silvery fish
And could swallow them down in a trice.

But Percy was very particular,
Particularly at lunch,
That the head of the fish was his part,
He didn't like tails to munch.

And Polly was very particular,
Particularly at midday,
That the tail of the fish was the best bit,
The heads she would just give away.

So, if ever you see two penguins
Holding fish in their flippers to slice;
It's sure to be Percy and Polly
Who live where the seas are ice.

Q q

Por-<u>Q</u>-pine

Por-**Q**-pines are prickly,
It's very plain to see
A por-**Q**-pine is not a
Comfy object on your knee.

His quills are very pointed,
They shiver and they snap
And dig into your tummy
If he fidgets on your lap.

He always seems to wriggle
Sending shivers up each spine,
So it's very hard to cuddle
The prickly por-**Q**-pine.

R r

Rabbits

Radishes are relished by rabbits for their lunch,
Radishes are really rich and wonderful to crunch.
The rabbit who eats radishes
Will grow enormous ears
That pick up sound and bounce around
Everything he hears.

Cabbage, crisp and crackly, is better for the feet,
It makes a rabbit's toes grow until they nearly meet.
The rabbit who eats radishes,
With cabbage crisp to follow
Can jump a stile and hear a mile
For every single swallow.

S s

Snail

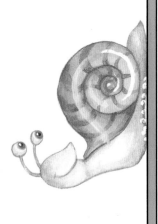

The snail is so slow, so slow, so slow,

He takes longer to go, to go, to go,

The hill is so steep, so steep, so steep,

And snail he must creep, must creep, must creep,

But snail is so strong, so strong, so strong,

Though it takes oh so long, so long, so long,

He'll win in the end, the end, the end,

The top's round the bend, the bend, the bend,

He's climbed all the way, today, hooray!

Now surely he'll stay, he'll stay, he'll stay,

But he's turning to go, oh no! Oh no!

To climb back below, below, below,

The snail is so slow, so slow, so slow!

T t

Tiger

A tiger is a fiery gold
With stripes as black as night,
Like bars across a furnace
As his skin and eyes glow bright.
He's frighteningly fierce
When he prowls and growls and roars,
But then, just like a kitten,
He will sit and wash his paws.

U u

Unicorn

Of all the birds and beasts and fishes
There's only one that grants you wishes,
This creature is the unicorn
With wishes in its magic horn.

The trouble with a horn is that
It makes it hard to wear a hat,
So unicorns are rarely found
With hoods or caps or bonnets round.

But when it's cold and snow lies deep,
A tight-wrapped scarf will sometimes keep
The magic warm inside the horn
So lots more wishes can be born.

V v

Vampire Bat

Oh vampire, oh vampire,
What an odd beast
And what a strange way
You have chosen to feast!
You really like blood? You funny old bat!
And you hang upside down? Just fancy that!

I don't think I'd like
To live in a cave
And sleep in the blackness
As dark as the grave;
You see with your ears? You really do?
I am glad I am me – not funny old you!

W w

Whale

The wallowing whale wheels in the sea
To make his great voyages, wild and free,
He stirs up the ocean, he leaps through the spray
Spouting fountains of water, he's so happy today!

The wallowing whale sings in the sea
A great sweep of notes, a strange melody,
It's a magical sound as he travels along,
Sending wave after wave of rippling song.

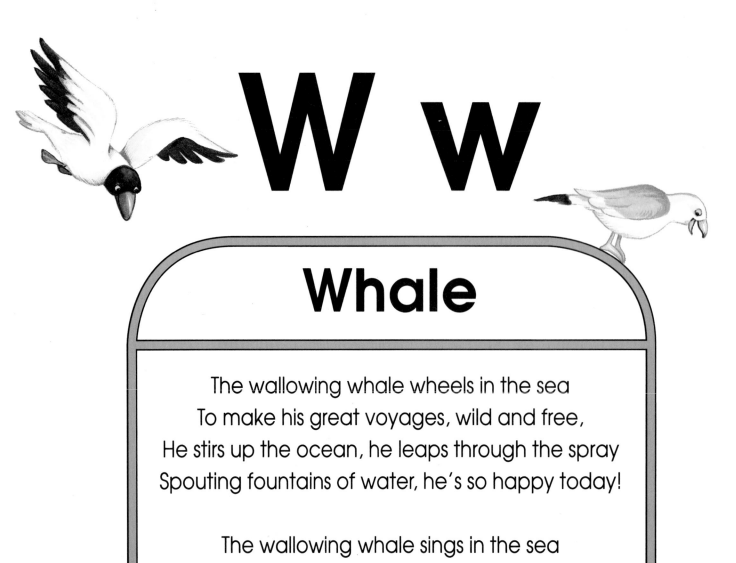

X x

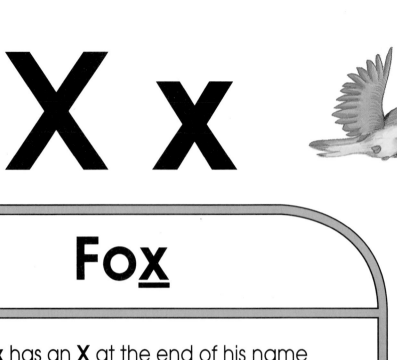

Fo<u>x</u>

The fo**x** has an **X** at the end of his name
And a tail at the end of his back,
The **X** has straight lines but his tail has a wave
And bobs as he runs down the track.

The fo**x** has an **X** at the end of his name
His tail-end is a beautiful red,
It's an excellent way to finish a fo**x**
At the opposite end to his head!

Y y

Yeti

When you climb the Himalayas
Or trot around Tibet,
Beware of looming shadows
After sun has set.

For where the snow has fallen
Footprints may appear,
It's not the cold that makes you shake
Or howl of wind you hear.

The Abominable Snowman,
Half-seen through swirling mists,
He lumbers through the blizzard
And across the snowy drifts.

They call this giant the yeti
I'm not sure if it's true,
But next time you climb Everest
Watch out! He's watching you!

Z z

Zebra

Are zebras always black and white?
Perhaps you think it's so,
But let me tell you of a zebra
I knew long ago.

This zebra said, ``My stripes are dull,
I want yellow, green and red!''
So he painted those that he could reach
From his tail up to his head.

But when the others saw his stripes
They laughed at him and shrieked,
``What a sight! You look just like
A pot of paint that's leaked!''

A a

B b

E e

F f

I i

J j

M m

N n

Q q

R r

U u

V v

Y y

C c

D d

G g

H h

K k

L l

O o

P p

S s

T t

W w

X x

Z z